AF576598

WATCHMAN NEE

God's Plan and God's Rest

Living Stream Ministry
Anaheim, California

ISBN 1-57593-863-4

Living Stream Ministry
1853 W. Ball Road, Anaheim, CA 92804 USA
P. O. Box 2121, Anaheim, CA 92814 USA

97 98 99 00 01 / 9 8 7 6 5 4 3 2 1

GOD'S PLAN AND GOD'S REST

Scripture Reading: Gen. 1:26—2:3; 2:18-24; Eph. 5:22-32; Rev. 12; 21:1—22:5

Four women are mentioned in these four passages of the Scriptures. In Genesis 2 the woman is Eve; in Ephesians 5 she is the church; in Revelation 12 she is the woman seen in the vision; and in Revelation 21 she is the wife of the Lamb.

May God grant us light to see how these four women are related to one another and to His eternal plan. Then we may see the position the church occupies and the responsibility she bears in this plan and how the overcomers of God will accomplish His eternal purpose.

GOD'S PURPOSE IN CREATING MAN

Why did God create man? What was His purpose in creating man?

God has given us the answer to these questions in Genesis 1:26 and 27. These two verses are of great significance. They reveal to us that God's creation of man was indeed an exceedingly special one. Before God created man, He said, "Let us make man in our image, after our likeness: and let them have dominion over the fish of the sea, and over the fowl of the air, and over the cattle, and over all the earth, and over every creeping thing that creepeth upon the earth." This was God's plan in creating man. "God said, Let us...." This speaks of the kind of man God wanted. In other words, God was designing a "model" for the man He was to create. Verse 27 reveals God's creation of man: "So God created man in his own image, in the image of God created he him; male and female created he them." Verse 28 says, "God blessed them, and God said unto them, Be fruitful, and multiply, and replenish the earth, and subdue it: and have dominion over the fish of the sea, and over the fowl of the air, and over every living thing that moveth upon the earth."

From these verses we see the man that God desired. God desired a ruling man, a man who would rule upon this earth; then He would be satisfied.

How did God create man? He created man in His own image. God wanted a man like Himself. It is very evident then that man's position in God's creation is entirely unique, for among all of God's creatures man alone was created in God's image. The man that God's heart was set upon was completely different from all other created beings; he was a man in His own image.

We notice here something quite remarkable. Verse 26 says, "Let us make man in *our* image, after *our* likeness..."; but verse 27 says, "So God created man in *his* own image, in the image of God created he him; male and female created he them." In verse 26 the pronoun "our" is plural, but in verse 27 "his" is singular. During the conference of the Godhead, verse 26 says, "Let us make man in *our* image"; therefore, according to grammar, verse 27 should say, "So God created man in *their* own image." But strangely, verse 27 says, "So God created man in *his* own image." How can we explain this? It is because there are three in the Godhead—the Father, the Son, and the Spirit, yet only one has the image in the Godhead—the Son. When the Godhead was designing man's creation, the Bible indicates that man would be made in "our" image (since They are one, "our image" was mentioned); but when the Godhead was in the actual process of making man, the Bible says that man was made in "his" image. "His" denotes the Son. From this we ascertain that Adam was made in the image of the Lord Jesus. Adam did not precede the Lord Jesus; the Lord Jesus preceded him. When God created Adam, He created him in the image of the Lord Jesus. It is for this reason it says "in his image" rather than "in their image."

God's purpose is to gain a group of people who are like His Son. When we read Romans 8:29 we find God's purpose: "Because those whom He foreknew, He also *predestinated* to be conformed to the image of His Son, that He might be the Firstborn among many brothers." God desires to have many sons, and God desires all these sons to be like that one Son of His. Then His Son will no more be the only Begotten, but the Firstborn among many brethren. God's desire is to gain such a group of people. If we see this, we will realize the preciousness of man, and we will rejoice whenever man is mentioned. How God values man! Even He Himself became a man! God's plan is to gain man. When man is gained by God, God's plan is accomplished.

It is by man that God's plan is fulfilled, and through man His own need is met. What, then, does God require from the man whom He created? It is that man should rule. When God created man, He did not predestine man to fall. Man's fall is in chapter three of Genesis, not chapter one. In God's plan to create man, He did not predestine man to sin, neither did He foreordain redemption. We are not minimizing the importance of redemption, but only saying that redemption was not foreordained by God. If it were, then man would have to sin. God did not foreordain this. In God's plan to create man, man was ordained to rule. This is revealed to us in Genesis 1:26. Here God unveils to us His desire and tells us the secret of His plan. "Let us make man in our image, after our likeness: and let them have dominion over the fish of the sea, and over the fowl of the air, and over the cattle, and over all the earth, and over every creeping thing that creepeth upon the earth." This is God's purpose in creating man.

Perhaps some may ask why God has such a purpose. It is because an angel of light rebelled against God before man's creation and became the devil: Satan sinned and fell; the Daystar became the enemy of God (Isa. 14:12-15). God, therefore, withdrew His authority from the enemy and put it, instead, into the hand of man. The reason God created man is that man may rule in the place of Satan. What abounding grace we see in God's creation of man!

Not only does God desire that man should rule, but He marks out a specific area for man to rule. We see this in Genesis 1:26: "Let them have dominion over the fish of the sea, and over the fowl of the air, and over the cattle, and over all the earth...." "All the earth" is the domain of man's rule. Not only did God give man dominion over the fish of the sea, the birds of the heavens, and the cattle, but He further required that man should rule over "all the earth." The area where God desired man to rule is the earth. Man is especially related to the earth. Not only in His plan to create man was God's attention focused upon the earth, but after God made man, He clearly told him that he was to rule over the earth. Verses 27 and 28 say, "So God created man in his own image, in the image of God created he him; male and female created he them. And God blessed them, and God said unto them, Be fruitful, and multiply, and replenish the earth, and subdue it...." What God emphasized here is that man should "replenish the earth" and "subdue it"; it is of secondary importance that man should have dominion over the fish of the sea, the fowl of the air, and every living thing on the earth. Man's dominion over these other things is an accessory; the main subject is the earth.

Genesis 1:1-2 says, "In the beginning God created the heavens and the earth. And the earth was waste and void; and darkness was upon the face of the deep" [ASV]. These two verses are made more clear by translating them directly from the Hebrew. According to the original language, verse one says, "In the beginning God created the heavens and the earth." The heavens here are plural in number and refer to the heavens of all the stars. (The earth has its heaven, and so do all the stars.) The direct translation of verse two is: "And the earth became [not "was"] waste and void; and darkness was upon the face of the deep." In Hebrew, preceding "the earth" there is the conjunction "and." "In the beginning God created the heavens and the earth"; there were no difficulties, no problems, but then something happened: "and the earth became waste and void." The word "was" in Genesis 1:2 ("And the earth was waste and void") and the word "became" in Genesis 19:26, where Lot's wife became a pillar of salt, are the same. Lot's wife was not born a pillar of salt; she became a pillar of salt. The earth was not waste and void at the creation, but later became waste and void. God created the heavens and the earth, but "the earth became waste and void." This reveals that the problem is not with the heavens but with the earth.

We see then that the earth is the center of all problems. God contends for the earth. The Lord Jesus taught us to pray, "Your name be sanctified; Your kingdom come; Your will be done, as in heaven, so also on *earth*" (Matt. 6:9-10). According to the meaning of the original language, the phrase "as in heaven, so also on earth" is common to all three clauses, not only to the last clause. In other words, the original meaning is: "Your name be sanctified, as in heaven, so also on earth. Your kingdom come, as in heaven, so also on earth. Your will be done, as in heaven, so also on earth." This prayer reveals that there is no problem with "heaven"; the problem is with the "earth." After the fall of man, God spoke to the serpent, "Upon thy belly shalt thou go, and dust shalt thou eat all the days of thy life" (Gen. 3:14). This meant that the earth would be the serpent's sphere, the place upon which he would creep. The realm of Satan's work is not heaven, but earth. If the kingdom of God is to come, then Satan must be cast out. If God's will is to be done, it must be done on earth. If God's name is to be sanctified, it must be sanctified on earth. All the problems are on the earth.

Two words in Genesis are very meaningful. One is "subdue" in Genesis 1:28, which can also be translated "conquer." The other is "keep" in Genesis 2:15, which can also be translated "guard." We see from these verses that God ordained man to conquer and guard the earth. God's original intention was to give the earth to man as a place to dwell. It was not His intention that the earth would become desolate (Isa. 45:18). God desired, through man, to not allow Satan to intrude upon the earth, but the problem was that Satan was on earth and intended to do a work of destruction upon it. Therefore, God wanted man to restore the earth from Satan's hand.

Another matter we need to note is that God required man, strictly speaking, not only to take back the earth, but also the heaven which is related to the earth. In the Scripture there is a difference between "heavens" and "heaven." The "heavens" are where the throne of God is found, where God can exercise His authority, while "heaven" in the Scriptures sometimes refers to the heaven which is related to the earth. It is this heaven which God also wants to recover (see Rev. 12:7-10).

Some may ask: Why doesn't God Himself cast Satan into the bottomless pit or the lake of fire? Our answer is: God can do it, but He does not want to do it Himself. We do not know why He will not do it Himself, but we do know how He is going to do it. God wants to use man to deal with His enemy, and He created man for this purpose. God wants the creature to deal with the creature. He wants His creature *man* to deal with His fallen creature *Satan* in order to bring the earth back to God. The man whom He created is being used by Him for this purpose.

Let us read Genesis 1:26 again: "And God said, Let us make man in our image, after our likeness: and let them have dominion over the fish of the sea, and over the fowl of the air, and over the cattle, and over all the earth...." It seems that the sentence is finished here, but another phrase is added: "...and over every creeping thing that creepeth upon the earth." Here we see that the creeping things occupy a very great position, for God spoke of it after He finished mentioning "all the earth." The implication is that in order for man to have dominion over all the earth, the creeping things must not be overlooked, for God's enemy is embodied in the creeping things. The serpent in Genesis 3 and the scorpions in Luke 10 are creeping things. Not only is there the serpent, representing Satan, but also scorpions, representing the sinful and unclean evil spirits. The domain of both the serpent and the scorpion is this earth. The problem is on the earth.

Therefore, we must distinguish the difference between the work of saving souls and the work of God. Many times the work of saving souls is not necessarily the work of God. Saving souls solves the problem of man, but the work of God requires that man exercise authority to have dominion over all things created by Him. God needs an authority in His creation, and He has chosen man to be that authority. If we were here just for ourselves as mere men, then all our seeking and longing would be to love the Lord more and to be more holy, more zealous, and save more souls. All of these pursuits are good indeed, but they are too man-centered. These things are concerned simply with the benefit of man; God's work and God's need are entirely neglected. We must see that God has His need. We are on this earth not merely for man's need but even more for God's need. Thank God that He has committed the ministry of reconciliation to us, but even if we have saved all the souls in the whole world, we have not yet accomplished God's work or satisfied God's requirement. Here is something called God's work, God's need. When God created man, He spoke of what He needed. He revealed His need to have man rule and reign over all His creation and proclaim His triumph. Ruling for God is not a small thing; it is a great matter. God needs men whom He can trust and who will not fail Him. This is God's work, and this is what God desires to obtain.

We do not lightly esteem the work of gospel preaching, but if all our work is just preaching the gospel and saving souls, we are not causing Satan to suffer fatal loss. If man has not restored the earth from the hand of Satan, he has not yet achieved God's purpose in creating him. Saving souls is often only for the welfare of man, but dealing with Satan is for the benefit of God. Saving souls solves man's need, but dealing with Satan satisfies God's need.

Brothers and sisters, this requires us to pay a price. We know how the demons can speak. A demon once said, "Jesus I know of, and with Paul I am acquainted; but who are you?" (Acts 19:15). When a demon meets us, will he flee or not? Preaching the gospel demands that we pay a price, but a much greater price must be paid to deal with Satan.

This is not a matter of a message or a teaching. This requires our practice, and the price is extremely great. If we are to be men whom God will use to overthrow all of Satan's work and authority, we must obey the Lord completely and absolutely!

In doing other work it matters less if we preserve ourselves a little, but when dealing with Satan, we cannot leave one bit of ground for ourselves. We may hold on to something of ourselves in our study of the Scriptures, in preaching the gospel, in helping the church or the brothers, but when we are dealing with Satan, self must be utterly abandoned. Satan will never be moved by us if self is preserved. May God open our eyes to see that His purpose demands that we be wholly and absolutely for Him. A double-minded person can never deal with Satan. May God speak this word to our hearts.

THE UNCHANGEABLE PURPOSE OF GOD

God wanted to have man to rule for Him on this earth, but man did not attain to God's purpose. In Genesis 3 the fall took place and sin entered; man came under the power of Satan, and everything seemed to come to an end. Satan was seemingly victorious and God was seemingly defeated. In addition to the passage in Genesis 1, there are two more passages in the Scriptures which are related to this problem. They are Psalm 8 and Hebrews 2.

PSALM 8

Psalm 8 shows that God's purpose and plan have never changed. After the fall, God's will and requirement for man remained the same without any alteration. His will in Genesis 1, when He created man, still holds good, even though man has sinned and fallen. Even though Psalm 8 was written after man's fall, the psalmist was able to praise; his eyes were still set upon Genesis 1. The Holy Spirit did not forget Genesis 1, the Son did not forget Genesis 1, nor did God Himself forget Genesis 1.

Let us see the content of this psalm. Verse 1 says:

> O Jehovah our Lord,
> How excellent is Your name
> In all the earth.

All who are inspired by the Holy Spirit will utter such words: "How excellent is Your name in all the earth!" Though some people slander and reject the Lord's name, yet the psalmist loudly proclaimed, "O Jehovah our Lord, how excellent is Your name in all the earth." He did not say, "Your name is very excellent." "Very excellent" does not have the same meaning as "how excellent." "Very excellent" means that I, the psalmist, can still describe the excellence, whereas "how excellent" means that even though I can write psalms, I do not have the words to express, nor do I know how excellent is the Lord's name. So I can only say, "O Jehovah our Lord, how excellent is Your name in all the earth!" Not only is His name excellent, His name is excellent "in all the earth"! The expression "in all the earth" is the same as in Genesis 1:26. If we know God's plan, every time we read the word "man" or the word "earth" our hearts should leap within us.

Verse 2 continues:

> Out of the mouths of babes
> and sucklings
> You have established strength
> Because of Your adversaries,
> To stop the enemy and the
> avenger.

Babes and sucklings refer to man, and the emphasis in this verse is upon God using man to deal with the enemy. The Lord Jesus quoted this verse in Matthew 21:16: "Out of the mouth of infants and sucklings You have perfected praise." These words mean that the enemy may do all he can, but it is not necessary for God Himself to deal with him. God will use babes and sucklings to deal with him. What can babes and sucklings do? It says, “Out of the mouths of babes and sucklings You have established strength.” God’s desire is to obtain men who are able to praise; those who can praise are those who can deal with the enemy.

In verses 3 through 8 the psalmist says:

When I see Your heavens,
the works of Your fingers,
The moon and the stars,
which You have ordained,
What is man, that You
remember him,
And the son of man, that You
visit him?
You have made him somewhat
lower than angels
And have crowned him with
glory and honor.
For You have caused him to rule
over the works of Your hands;
You have put all things under
his feet:
All sheep and oxen,
As well as the beasts of the
field,

The birds of heaven and the fish
of the sea,
Whatever passes through the
paths of the seas.

If we were writing this psalm, perhaps we would add a parentheses at this point: "How pitiful that man has fallen and sinned and been cast out of the garden of Eden! No more can man attain to this." But thank God, in the heart of the psalmist there was not such a thought. In God's view the earth can still be restored, the position given to man by God still exists, and His commitment to man to destroy the work of the devil still remains. Therefore, starting from the third verse, the psalmist again narrates the same old story, completely ignoring the third chapter of Genesis. This is the outstanding feature of Psalm 8. God's purpose is for man to rule. Is man worthy? Certainly not! But since God's purpose is for man to rule, man will surely rule.

In verse 9 the psalmist again says,

O Jehovah our Lord,
How excellent is Your name
In all the earth!

He continues to praise, as though he were not even aware of man's fall. Though

Adam had sinned and Eve had also sinned, they could never withstand God's plan. Man can fall and man can sin, but man cannot overthrow the will of God. Even after man fell, God's will toward man remained the same. God still requires man to overthrow the power of Satan. Oh, what an unchangeable God He is! His way is unswerving and utterly straightforward. We must realize that God can never be overthrown. In this world there are some who receive many hard blows, but no one has been attacked daily and received continual blasts like God. Yet His will has never been overthrown. What God was before man's fall, He is after man's fall and after sin entered into the world. The decision He affirmed aforetime is still His decision today. He has never changed.

HEBREWS 2

Genesis 1 speaks of the will of God at creation, Psalm 8 speaks of God's will after man's fall, and Hebrews 2 speaks of God's will in redemption. Let us look at Hebrews 2. We will see that in the victory of redemption God still desires man to obtain authority and deal with Satan.

In verses 5 through 8a the writer says, "For it was not to angels that He subjected the coming inhabited earth, concerning which we speak. But one has solemnly testified somewhere, saying, 'What is man, that You bring him to mind? Or the son of man, that You care for him? You have made Him a little inferior to the angels; You have crowned Him with glory and honor and have set Him over the works of Your hands; You have subjected all things under His feet' [quoted from Psalm 8]. For in subjecting all things to Him, He left nothing unsubject to Him." All things must be subject to man; God purposed it from the beginning.

But it has not yet turned out in this way. The writer continues, "But now we do not yet see all things subjected to Him, but we see Jesus, who was made a little inferior to the angels because of the suffering of death, crowned with glory and honor" (vv. 8b-9a). Jesus is the person who fits this situation. Psalm 8 said that God made man a little lower than the angels, but the apostle changed the word "man" into "Jesus." He explained that "man" refers to Jesus; it was Jesus who became a little lower than the angels. Man's redemption is by Him. God originally purposed that man should be a little lower than the angels and that man should be crowned and rule over all His creation. He intended for man to exercise authority on His behalf to cast out His enemy from the earth and from the heaven related to the earth. He wanted man to destroy all of Satan's power. But man fell and did not take his place to rule. Therefore, the Lord Jesus came and took upon Him a body of flesh and blood. He became the "last Adam" (1 Cor. 15:45).

The last part of verse 9 says, "So that by the grace of God He might taste death on behalf of everything." The birth of the Lord Jesus, the human living of the Lord Jesus, as well as the redemption of the Lord Jesus show us that His redemptive work is not only for man, but for all created things. All creation (except the angels) is included. The Lord Jesus stood in two positions: to God He was the man at the beginning, the man whom God appointed from the very first, and to man He is the Savior. In the beginning God assigned man to rule and overthrow Satan. The Lord Jesus is that man, and that man is now enthroned! Hallelujah! Such a man has overthrown the power of Satan. He is the man whom God is after and desires to obtain. In His other aspect, He is a man related to us; He is our Savior, the One who has dealt with the problem of sin in our place. We sinned and fell, and God made Him to be the propitiation for us. Furthermore, He not only became the propitiation for us, but He was also judged for all creatures. This is proved by the splitting of the veil in the holy place. Hebrews 10 tells us that the veil in the holy place signified the body of the Lord Jesus. Upon the veil were embroidered cherubim, which represent created things. At the time of the Lord's death, the veil was split in two from the top to the bottom; as a result, the cherubim embroidered upon it were simultaneously rent. This reveals that the death of the Lord Jesus included judgment for all creatures. He not only tasted death for every man, but also for "everything."

Verse 10 continues, "For it was fitting for Him, for whom are all things and through whom are all things, in leading many sons into glory." All things are for Him and through Him; all things are to Him and by Him. To be for Him means to be to Him; to be through Him means to be by Him. Praise God, He has not changed His purpose in creation! What God ordained at creation He continued to ordain after man's fall. In redemption His purpose remains the same. God did not change His purpose because of man's fall. Praise God, He is bringing many sons into glory! He is glorifying many sons. God purposed to gain a group of new men who have the likeness and the image of His Son. Since the Lord Jesus is the representative man, the rest will be like whatever He is, and they will enter with Him into glory.

How is this to be accomplished? Verse 11 says, "For both He who sanctifies and those who are being sanctified are all of One." Who is He that sanctifies? It is the Lord Jesus. Who are those that are being sanctified? We are the ones. We can read the verse in this way: "For both Jesus who sanctifies and we who are sanctified are all of One." The Lord Jesus and we are all begotten of the same Father; we have all originated from the same source and have the same life. We have the same indwelling Spirit and the same God, who is our Lord and our Father. "For which cause He is not ashamed to call them brothers." The word "He" refers to our Lord Jesus, and "them" to us. "He is not ashamed to call them brothers" because He is of the Father and we also are of the Father.

We are God's many sons, which will ultimately result in God bringing us into glory. Redemption did not change God's purpose; on the contrary, it fulfilled the purpose that was not accomplished in creation. God's original purpose was that man should rule, especially over the earth, but man regrettably failed. Yet all things did not come to an end because of the first man's fall. What God did not obtain from the first man, Adam, He will obtain from the second man, Christ. There was the eventful birth in Bethlehem because God ordained man to rule and restore the earth and because God determined that the creature man should destroy the creature Satan. This is why the Lord Jesus came to become a man. He did it purposely, and He became a true man. The first man did not accomplish God's purpose; rather, he sinned and fell. He not only failed to restore the earth, but he was captured by Satan. He not only failed to rule, but he was brought into subjection to Satan's power. Genesis 2 says that man was made of dust, and Genesis 3 points out that dust was the food of the serpent. This means that fallen man became the food of Satan. Man could no longer deal with Satan; he was finished. What could be done? Did this mean that God could never achieve His eternal purpose, that He could no longer obtain what He was after? Did it mean that God could never restore the earth? No! He sent His Son to become a man. The Lord Jesus is truly God, but He is also truly man.

In the whole world there is at least one man who chooses God, a person who can say, "The ruler of the world is coming, and in Me he has nothing" (John 14:30). In other words, in the Lord Jesus there is not a trace of the prince of this world. We must note carefully that the Lord Jesus came to this world not to be God but to be man. God required a man. If God Himself dealt with Satan, it would be very easy; Satan would fall in a moment. But God would not do it Himself. He wanted man to deal with Satan; He intended that the creature would deal with the creature. When the Lord Jesus became a man, He suffered temptation as a man and passed through all the experiences of man. This man conquered; this man was victorious. He ascended to heaven and sat down at the right hand of God. Jesus has been "crowned with glory and honor" (Heb. 2:9). He has been glorified.

He did not come to receive glory as God, but to obtain glory as man. We do not mean that He did not have the glory of God, but Hebrews 2 does not refer to the glory which He possessed as God. It refers to Jesus, who was made a little lower than the angels because of the suffering of death; Jesus was crowned with glory and honor. Our Lord ascended as a man. Today He is in the heavens as man. A man is at God's right hand. In the future there will be many men who will be there. Today a man is sitting on the throne. One day there will be many men sitting on the throne. This is certain.

When the Lord Jesus was resurrected, He imparted His life into us. When we believe in Him, we receive His life. We all become God's sons, and as such, we all belong to God. Because we have this life within us, as men we can be entrusted by God to fulfill His purpose. Therefore, it says that He will bring many sons into glory. To rule is to be glorified, and to be glorified is to rule. When the many sons have obtained authority and restored the earth, then they will be brought triumphantly into glory.

We should never presume that God's purpose is merely to save us from hell that we may enjoy the blessings of heaven. We must remember that God intends for man to follow His Son in the exercise of His authority on the earth. God wants to accomplish something, but He will not do it Himself; He wants us to do it. When we have done it, then God will have attained His purpose. God desires to obtain a group of men who will do His work here on this earth, that God may rule on earth through man.

THE RELATIONSHIP BETWEEN REDEMPTION AND CREATION

We need to note the relationship between redemption and creation. We should by no means consider that the Bible speaks of nothing but redemption. Thank God that in addition to redemption there is also creation. The desire of God's heart is expressed in creation. God's goal, God's plan, and God's predetermined will are all made known in His creation. Creation reveals God's eternal purpose; it shows us what God is truly after.

The place of redemption cannot be higher than that of creation. What is redemption? Redemption recovers what God did not obtain through creation. Redemption does not bring anything new to us; it only restores to us what is already ours. God through redemption achieves His purpose in creation. To redeem means to restore and recover; to create means to determine and initiate. Redemption is something afterward, so that God's purpose in creation may be fulfilled. Oh, that the Lord's children would not despise creation, thinking that redemption is everything. Redemption is related to us; it benefits us by saving us and bringing us eternal life. But creation is related to God and God's work. Our relationship with redemption is for the benefit of man, while our relationship with creation is for the economy of God. May God do a new thing on this earth, so that man will not only stress the gospel but go beyond that to take care of God's work, God's affairs, and God's plan. In fact, our preaching of the gospel should be with a view to bringing the earth back to God. We must show Christ's triumph over the kingdom of Satan. If we are not Christians, that is something else. But once we have become Christians, we should not only receive the benefit of redemption but also achieve God's purpose in creation. Without redemption we could never be related to God. But once we have been saved, we need to offer ourselves to God to attain the goal for which He first made man. If we pay attention only to the gospel, that is only half of the matter. God requires the other half, that man may rule for Him upon the earth and not allow Satan to remain here any longer. This half is also required of the church. Hebrews 2 shows us that redemption is not only for the forgiveness of sins, that man may be saved, but also to restore man back to the purpose of creation.

Redemption is comparable to the valley between two peaks. As one descends from one peak and proceeds to ascend the other, he encounters redemption at the lowest part of the valley. To redeem simply means to prevent man from falling any further and to uplift him. On the one hand, God's will is eternal and straightforward, without any dip, so that the purpose of creation may be achieved. On the other hand, something happened. Man has fallen, and man has departed from God. The distance between him and God's eternal purpose has become farther and farther apart. God's will from eternity to eternity is a straight line, but ever since his fall, man has not been able to attain to it. Thank God, there is a remedy called redemption. When redemption came, man did not need to go down anymore. After redemption man is changed and begins to ascend. As man continues to rise the day will come when he will again touch the one straight line. The day that line is reached is the day the kingdom will come.

We thank God that we have redemption. Apart from it we would plunge lower and lower; we would be suppressed by Satan more and more until there would be no way to rise. Praise God, redemption has caused us to return to God's eternal purpose. What God did not obtain in creation and what man lost in the fall are completely regained in redemption.

We must ask God to open our eyes to see what He has done so that our living and work may have a real turn. If all our work is just to save others, we are still a failure, and we cannot satisfy God's heart. Both redemption and creation are for the obtaining of glory and the overthrowing of all the power of the devil. Let us proclaim the love of God and the authority of God as we see the sin and the fall of man. But at the same time, we must exercise spiritual authority to overthrow the devil's power. The commission of the church is twofold: to testify the salvation of Christ and to testify the triumph of Christ. On the one hand, the church is to bring benefit to man, and on the other hand, it is to cause Satan to suffer loss.

GOD'S REST

In all six days of God's work of creation, His creation of man was distinct. All His work throughout the six days was for this. His real aim was to create man. In order to do this, God first had to repair the ruined earth and heaven. (Genesis 2:4 says, "These are the generations of the heavens and of the earth when they were created, in the day that the Lord God made the earth and the heavens." "The heavens and the earth" refer to the creation in the beginning, since at that time it was the heavens that were first formed and then the earth. But the second part, "in the day that the Lord God made the earth and the heavens," refers to His repair and restoration work, since in this work the earth was cared for first and then the heaven.) After God restored the ruined earth and heaven, He created the man of His design. After the sixth day, there was the seventh day; on this day God rested from all His work.

Rest comes after work: work must be first, and then rest may follow. Moreover, work must be completed to entire satisfaction before there can be any rest. If the work has not been done completely and satisfactorily, there can never be any rest to the mind or heart. We should not, therefore, esteem lightly the fact that God rested after six days of creation. For God to rest is a great matter. It was necessary for Him to have gained a certain objective before He could rest. How great the power must be which moved such a Creator God to rest! To cause such a God, who plans so much and who is full of life, to enter into rest requires the greatest strength.

Genesis 2 shows us that God rested on the seventh day. How is it that God could rest? The end of Genesis 1 records that it was because "God saw every thing that he had made, and, behold, it was very good" (v. 31).

God rested on the seventh day. Before the seventh day, He had work to do, and prior to His work, He had a purpose. Romans 11 speaks of the mind of the Lord and His judgments and ways. Ephesians 1 speaks of the mystery of His will, His good pleasure, and His foreordained purpose. Ephesians 3 also speaks of His foreordained purpose. From these Scriptures we gather that God is not only a God who works, but a God who purposes and plans. When He delighted to work, He proceeded to work; He worked because He wished to work. When He found satisfaction with His work, He rested. If we desire to know God's will, His plan, His good pleasure, and His purpose, we have only to look at that which caused Him to rest. If we see that God rests in a certain thing, then we may know that is something He was originally after. Man too cannot rest in that which does not satisfy him; he must gain what he is after and then he will have rest. We must not regard this rest lightly, for its meaning is very great. God did not rest in the first six days, but He rested in the seventh day. His rest reveals that God accomplished His heart's desire. He did something which made Him rejoice. Therefore, He could rest.

We must note the word "behold" in Genesis 1:31. What is its meaning? When we have purchased a certain object with which we are particularly satisfied, we turn it around with pleasure and look it over well. This is what it means to behold. God did not just casually "look" upon all that He had made and see that it was good. Rather, He "beheld" everything which He had made and saw that it was very good. We need to take note that God was there at the creation "beholding" what He had made. The word "rested" is the declaration that God was satisfied, that God delighted in what He had done; it proclaims that God's purpose was attained and His good pleasure was accomplished to the fullest. His work was perfected to such an extent that it could not have been made better.

For this reason God commanded the Israelites to observe the Sabbath throughout their generations. God was after something. God was seeking something to satisfy Himself, and He attained it; therefore, He rested. This is the meaning of the Sabbath. It is not that man should purchase fewer things or walk less miles. The Sabbath tells us that God had a heart's desire, a requirement to satisfy Himself, and a work had to be done to fulfill His heart's desire and demand. Since God has obtained what He was after, He is at rest. It is not a matter of a particular day. The Sabbath tells us that God has fulfilled His plan, attained His goal, and satisfied His heart. God is One who demands satisfaction, and He is also One who can be satisfied. After God has what He desires, He rests.

What then brought rest to God? What was it that gave Him such satisfaction? During the six days of creation there were light, air, grass, herbs, and trees; there were the sun, the moon, and the stars; there were fish, birds, cattle, creeping things, and beasts. But in all these God did not find rest. Finally there was man, and God rested from all His work. All of the creation before man was preparatory. All of God's expectations were focused upon man. When God gained a man, He was satisfied and He rested.

Let us read Genesis 1:27-28 again: "So God created man in his own image, in the image of God created he him; male and female created he them. And God blessed them, and God said unto them, Be fruitful, and multiply, and replenish the earth, and subdue it: and have dominion over the fish of the sea, and over the fowl of the air, and over every living thing that moveth upon the earth." Now read Genesis 1:31 with Genesis 2:3: "And God saw every thing that he had made, and, behold, it was very good....And God blessed the seventh day, and sanctified it: because that in it he had rested from all his work which God created and made." God had a purpose, and this purpose was to gain man—man with authority to rule over the earth. Only the realization of this purpose could satisfy God's heart. If this could be obtained, all would be well. On the sixth day God's purpose was achieved. "God saw every thing that he had made, and, behold, it was very good...and he rested on the seventh day from all his work." God's purpose and expectation were attained; He could stop and rest. God's rest was based upon man who would rule.